DeerSteers

by Alison Wells

illustrations by Stephen Smock

Harcourt Brace & Company

Orlando   Atlanta   Austin   Boston   San Francisco   Chicago   Dallas   New York   Toronto   London

Moose and Deer pack their gear
for a trip to a lake that's near.
"Clear Lake, here we come!"
they cheer.

Deer shifts gears. The car rears. Moose wipes a tear as Deer steers!

Deer slows down when Clear Lake is near. Moose looks at the sign as Deer steers.

Soon Clear Lake appears.
Deer turns into a place
that's clear.

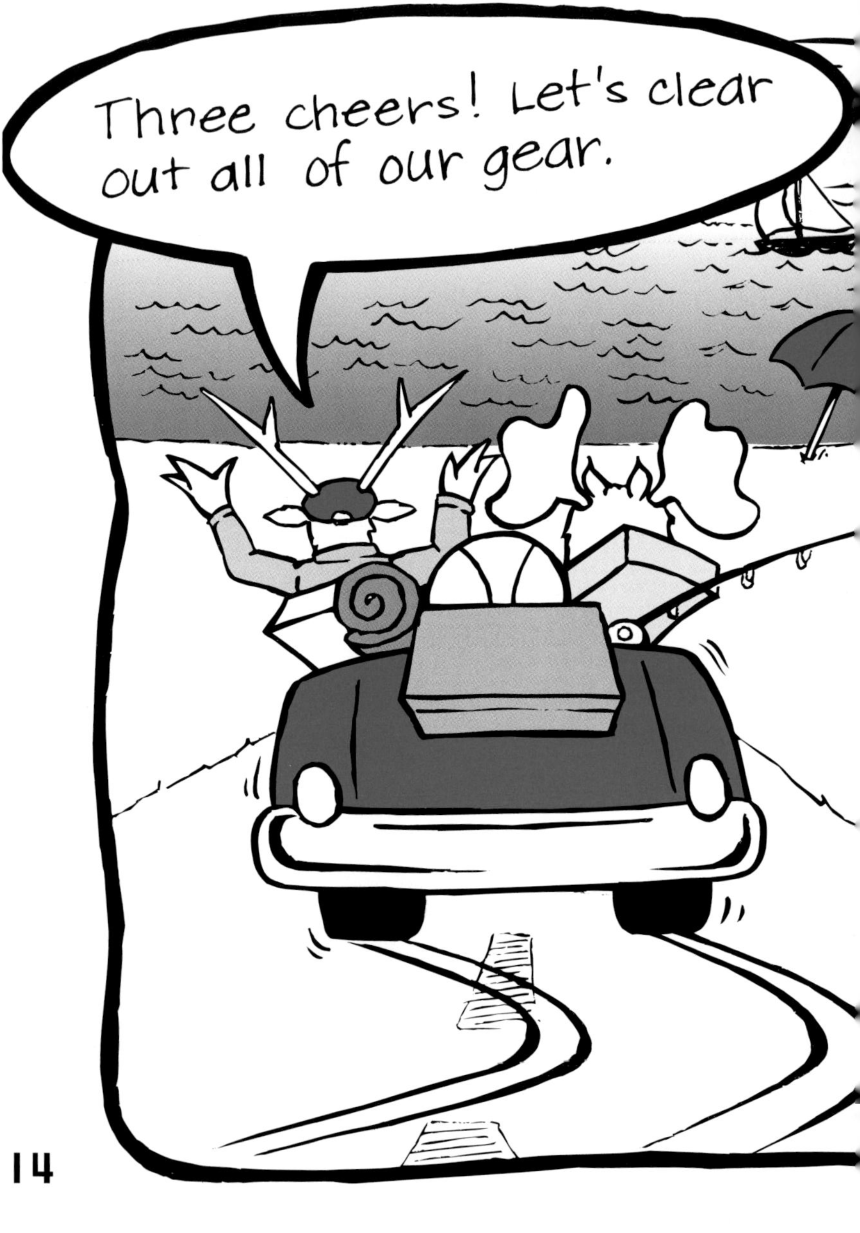
Three cheers! Let's clear out all of our gear.

Moose hears something,
and Deer looks as another
car appears.